OTHER PLACES

FOUR PLAYS BY
HAROLD PINTER

D1024184

★

DRAMATISTS
PLAY SERVICE
INC.

To Mick Goldstein

Other Places
A Kind of Alaska, Victoria Station, Family Voices

Other Places is a triple bill of short plays first presented at the National Theatre in autumn 1982.

A Kind of Alaska was, Pinter says, "inspired" by Oliver Sacks' book *Awakenings*, an account of Dr. Sacks' work with patients suffering from sleeping sickness.

Victoria Station concerns a minicab driver and his controller.

Family Voices, first heard on radio in 1981, is written for three people, a mother, her dead husband and her absent son.

In the New York production, by the Manhattan Theatre Club, *Family Voices* was replaced by *One For The Road.* Groups producing *Other Places* are free to use either combination of plays. (Or, if they wish, all four plays on one program.)

Please note, however, that when *A Kind of Alaska* is licensed for separate production, with a companion piece, the companion piece *must* be another play by Harold Pinter or a play approved by Mr. Pinter. In the latter situation, requests should be made in writing to the Play Service well in advance of projected production dates.

SPECIAL NOTE

All groups receiving permission to produce *A Kind Of Alaska* are required to include the following credit in all programs distributed in connection with performances of the play:

"This play was inspired by AWAKENINGS by Oliver Sacks MD."

OTHER PLACES was first performed in the Cottesloe auditorium of the National Theatre, London, on October 14, 1982 with the following cast:

FAMILY VOICES

VOICE 1 ....Nigel Havers
VOICE 2 .... Anna Massey
VOICE 3 ....Paul Rogers

VICTORIA STATION

CONTROLLER...Paul Rogers
DRIVER... Martin Jarvis

A KIND OF ALASKA

DEBORAH ....Judi Dench
HORNBY...Paul Rogers
PAULINE... Anna Massey

Directed by Peter Hall
Designed by John Bury

OTHER PLACES was presented by the Manhattan Theatre Club, in New York City, on April 17, 1984. (With FAMILY VOICES replaced by ONE FOR THE ROAD.) It was directed by Alan Schneider; the set design was by John Lee Beatty; the costume design was by Jess Goldstein; and the lighting design was by Rocky Greenberg. The cast was as follows:

VICTORIA STATION

CONTROLLER... Henderson Forsythe
DRIVER..Kevin Conway

ONE FOR THE ROAD

NICOLAS ....Kevin Conway
VICTOR .... Greg Martin
GILA ....Caroline Lagerfelt
NICKY ....David George Polyak

A KIND OF ALASKA

DEBORAH .... Dianne Wiest
HORNBY... Henderson Forsythe
PAULINE..Caroline Lagerfelt

CONTENTS

A KIND OF ALASKA

CHARACTERS

DEBORAH
HORNBY
PAULINE

A KIND OF ALASKA was inspired by *Awakenings* by Oliver Sacks M.D., first published in 1973 by Gerald Duckworth and Co.

In the winter of 1916-17, there spread over Europe, and subsequently over the rest of the world, an extraordinary epidemic illness which presented itself in innumerable forms — as delirium, mania, trances, coma, sleep, insomnia, restlessness, and states of Parkinsonism. It was eventually identified by the great physician Constantin von Economo and named by him *encephalitis lethargic,* or sleeping sickness.

Over the next ten years almost five million people fell victim to the disease of whom more than a third died. Of the survivors some escaped almost unscathed, but the majority moved into states of deepening illness. The worst-affected sank into singular states of "sleep" — conscious of their surroundings but motionless, speechless, and without hope or will, confined to asylums or other institutions.

Fifty years later, with the development of the remarkable drug L-DOPA, they erupted into life once more.

A KIND OF ALASKA

A woman in a white bed. Mid-forties. She sits up against
high-banked pillows, stares ahead.
A table and two chairs. A window.
A man in a dark suit sits at the table. Early sixties.
The woman's eyes move. She slowly looks about her.
Her gaze passes over the man and on.
He watches her.
She stares ahead, still.
She whispers.

DEBORAH. Something is happening. *(Silence.)*

HORNBY. Do you know me? *(Silence.)* Do you recognise me?
(Silence.) Can you hear me? *(She does not look at him.)*

DEBORAH. Are you speaking?

HORNBY. Yes. *(Pause.)* Do you know who I am? *(Pause.)* Who
am I?

DEBORAH. No-one hears what I say. No-one is listening to
me. *(Pause.)*

HORNBY. Do you know who I am? *(Pause.)* Who am I?

DEBORAH. You are no-one. *(Pause.)* Who is it? It is miles away.
The rain is falling. I will get wet. *(Pause.)* I can't get to sleep. The dog
keeps turning about. I think he's dreaming. He wakes me up, but not
himself up. He's my best dog though. I talk French. *(Pause.)*

HORNBY. I would like you to listen to me. *(Pause.)* You have been
asleep for a very long time. You have now woken up. We are here to
care for you. *(Pause.)* You have been asleep for a very long time. You
are older, although you do not know that. You are still young, but
older. *(Pause.)*

DEBORAH. Something is happening.

HORNBY. You have been asleep. You have awoken. Can you hear
me? Do you understand me? *(She looks at him for the first time.)*

DEBORAH. Asleep? *(Pause.)* I do not remember that. *(Pause.)*
People have been looking at me. They have been touching me. I
spoke, but I don't think they heard what I said. *(Pause.)* What
language am I speaking? I speak French, I know that. Is this French?
(Pause.) I've not seen Daddy today. He's funny. He makes me laugh.
He runs with me. We play with balloons. *(Pause.)* Where is he?
(Pause.) I think it's my birthday soon. *(Pause.)* No, no. No, no. I
sleep like other people. No more no less. Why should I? If I sleep
late my mother wakes me up. There are things to do. *(Pause.)* If I
have been asleep, why hasn't Mummy woken me up?
HORNBY. I have woken you up.
DEBORAH. But I don't know you. *(Pause.)* Where is everyone?
Where is my dog? Where are my sisters? Last night Estelle was
wearing my dress. But I said she could. *(Pause.)* I am cold.
HORNBY. How old are you?
DEBORAH. I am twelve. No. I am sixteen. I am seven. *(Pause.)* I
don't know. Yes. I know. I am fourteen. I am fifteen. I'm lovely
fifteen. *(Pause.)* You shouldn't have brought me here. My mother
will ask me where I've been. *(Pause.)* You shouldn't have touched
me like that. I shan't tell my mother. I shouldn't have touched you
like that. *(Pause.)* Oh Jack. *(Pause.)* It's time I was up and about. All
those dogs are making such a racket. I suppose Daddy's feeding
them. Is Estelle going to marry that boy from Townley Street? The
ginger boy? Pauline says he's got nothing between his ears. Thick as
two planks. I've given it a good deal of rather more mature thought
and I've decided she should not marry him. Tell her not to marry
him. She'll listen to you. *(Pause.)* Daddy?
HORNBY. She didn't marry him.
DEBORAH. Didn't? *(Pause.)* It would be a great mistake. It would
ruin her life.
HORNBY. She didn't marry him. *(Silence.)*
DEBORAH. I've seen this room before. What room is this? It's not
my bedroom. My bedroom has blue lilac on the walls. The sheets are
soft, pretty. Mummy kisses me. *(Pause.)* This is not my bedroom.
HORNBY. You have been in this room for a long time. You have
been asleep. You have now woken up.
DEBORAH. You shouldn't have brought me here. What are you
saying? Did I ask you to bring me here? Did I make eyes at you?
Did I show desire for you? Did I let you peep up my skirt? Did I
flash my teeth? Was I as bold as brass? Perhaps I've forgotten.

HORNBY. I didn't bring you here. Your mother and father brought you here.

DEBORAH. My father? My mother? *(Pause.)* Did they bring me to you as a sacrifice? Did they sacrifice me to you? *(Pause.)* No, no. You stole me … in the night. *(Pause.)* Have you had your way with me?

HORNBY. I am here to take care of you.

DEBORAH. They all say that. *(Pause.)* You've had your way with me. You made me touch you. You stripped me. I cried … but … but it was my lust made me cry. You are a devil. My lust was my own. I kept it by me. You took it from me. Once open never closed. Never closed again. Never closed always open. For eternity. Terrible. You have ruined me. *(Pause.)* I sound childish. Out of … tune. *(Pause.)* How old am I? *(Pause.)* Eighteen?

HORNBY. No.

DEBORAH. Well then, I've no idea how old I am. Do you know?

HORNBY. Not exactly.

DEBORAH. Why not? *(Pause.)* My sisters would know. We're very close. We love each other. We're known as the three bluebells. *(Pause.)* Why is everything so quiet? So still? I'm in a sandbag. The sea. Is that what I hear? A long way away. Gulls. Haven't heard a gull for ages. God what a racket. Where's Pauline? She's such a mischief. I have to keep telling her not to be so witty. That's what I say. You're too witty for your own good. You're so sharp you'll cut yourself. You're too witty for your own tongue. You'll bite your own tongue off one of these days and I'll keep your tongue in a closed jar and you'll never ever ever ever be witty again. *(Pause.)* She's all right, really. She just talks too much. Whereas Estelle is as deep as a pond. She's marvellous at crossing her legs. Sen-su-al. *(Pause.)* This is a hotel. A hotel near the sea. Hastings? Torquay? There's more to this than meets the eye. I'm coming to that conclusion. There's something very shady about you. Pauline always says I'll end up as part of the White Slave Traffic. *(Pause.)* Yes. This is a white tent. When I open the flap I'll step out into the Sahara Desert.

HORNBY. You've been asleep.

DEBORAH. Oh, you keep saying that! What's wrong with that? Why shouldn't I have a long sleep for a change? I need it. My body demands it. It's quite natural. I may have overslept but I didn't do it deliberately. If I had any choice in the matter I'd much prefer to be up and about. I love the morning. Why do you blame me? I was simply obeying the law of the body.

13

HORNBY. I know that. I'm not blaming you.

DEBORAH. Well, how long have I been asleep? *(Pause.)*

HORNBY. You have been asleep for twenty-nine years. *(Silence.)*

DEBORAH. You mean I'm dead?

HORNBY. No.

DEBORAH. I don't feel dead.

HORNBY. You're not.

DEBORAH. But you mean I've been dead?

HORNBY. If you had been dead you wouldn't be alive now.

DEBORAH. Are you sure?

HORNBY. No-one wakes from the dead.

DEBORAH. No, I shouldn't think so. *(Pause.)* Well, what was I doing if I wasn't dead?

HORNBY. We don't know … what you were doing.

DEBORAH. We? *(Pause.)* Where's my mother? My father? Estelle? Pauline?

HORNBY. Pauline is here. She's waiting to see you.

DEBORAH. She shouldn't be out at this time of night. I'm always telling her. She needs her beauty sleep. Like I do, by the way. But of course I'm her elder sister so she doesn't listen to me. And Estelle doesn't listen to me because she's my elder sister. That's family life. And Jack? Where's Jack? Where's my boyfriend? He's my boyfriend. He loves me. He loves me. I once saw him cry. For love. Don't make him cry again. What have you done to him? What have you done with him? What? What? What?

HORNBY. Be calm. Don't agitate yourself.

DEBORAH. Agitate myself?

HORNBY. There's no hurry about any of this.

DEBORAH. Any of what?

HORNBY. Be calm.

DEBORAH. I am calm. *(Pause.)* I've obviously committed a criminal offence and am now in prison. I'm quite prepared to face up to the facts. But what offence? I can't imagine what offence it could be. I mean one that would bring … such a terrible sentence.

HORNBY. This is not a prison. You have committed no offence.

DEBORAH. But what have I done? What have I been doing? Where have I been?

HORNBY. Do you remember nothing of where you've been? Do you remember nothing … of all that has happened to you?

DEBORAH. Nothing has happened to me. I've been nowhere. *(Silence.)*

HORNBY. I think we should —

DEBORAH. I certainly don't want to see Pauline. People don't want to see their sisters. They're only their sisters. They're so witty. All I hear is chump chump. The side teeth. Eating everything in sight. Gold chocolate. So greedy eat it with the paper on. Munch all the ratshit on the sideboard. Someone has to polish it off. Been there for years. Statues of excrement. Wrapped in gold. I've never got used to it. Sisters are diabolical. Brothers are worse. One day I prayed I would see no-one ever again, none of them ever again. All that eating, all that wit. *(Pause.)*

HORNBY. I didn't know you had any brothers.

DEBORAH. What? *(Pause.)*

HORNBY. Come. Rest. Tomorrow ... is another day.

DEBORAH. No it isn't. No it isn't. It is not! *(She smiles.)* Yes, of course it is. Of course it is. Tomorrow is another day. I'd love to ask you a question.

HORNBY. Are you not tired?

DEBORAH. Tired? Not at all. I'm wide awake. Don't you think so?

HORNBY. What is the question?

DEBORAH. How did you wake me up? *(Pause.)* Or did you not wake me up? Did I just wake up myself? All by myself? Or did you wake me with a magic wand?

HORNBY. I woke you with an injection.

DEBORAH. Lovely injection. Oh how I love it. And am I beautiful?

HORNBY. Certainly.

DEBORAH. And you are my Prince Charming. Aren't you? *(Pause.)* Oh speak up. *(Pause.)* Silly shit. All men are alike. *(Pause.)* I think I love you.

HORNBY. No, you don't.

DEBORAH. Well, I'm not spoilt for choice here, am I? There's not another man in sight. What have you done with all the others? There's a boy called Peter. We play with his trains, we play ... Cowboys and Indians ... I'm a tomboy. I knock him about. But that was ... *(Pause.)* But now I've got all the world before me. All life before me. All my life before me. *(Pause.)* I've had enough of this. Find Jack. I'll say yes. We'll have kids. I'll bake apples. I'm ready for it. No point in hanging about. Best foot forward. Mummy's motto. Bit of a cheek, I think, Mummy not coming in to say hullo, to say goodnight, to tuck me up, to sing me a song, to warn me about going too far with boys. Daddy I love but he is a bit absent-minded. Thinking of other things. That's what Pauline says. She says he has a mistress in Fulham. The bitch. I mean Pauline. And she's only ... thirteen. I keep telling her I'm not prepared to tolerate her risible, her tendentious, her eclectic, her ornate, her rococo insinuations and garbled inventions. I tell her that every day of the week. *(Pause.)* Daddy is kind and so is Mummy. We all have breakfast together every morning in the kitchen. What's happening? *(Pause.)*

HORNBY. One day suddenly you stopped.

DEBORAH. Stopped?

HORNBY. Yes. *(Pause.)* You fell asleep and no-one could wake you. But although I use the word sleep, it was not strictly sleep.

DEBORAH. Oh, make up your mind! *(Pause.)* You mean you thought I was asleep but I was actually awake?

HORNBY. Neither asleep nor awake.

DEBORAH. Was I dreaming?

HORNBY. Were you?

DEBORAH. Well was I? I don't know. *(Pause.)* I'm not terribly pleased about all this. I'm going to ask a few questions in a few minutes. One of them might be: What did I look like while I was asleep, or while I was awake, or whatever it was I was? Bet you can't tell me.

HORNBY. You were quite still. Fixed. Most of the time.

DEBORAH. Show me. *(Pause.)* Show me what I looked like. *(He demonstrates a still, fixed position. She studies him. She laughs, stops abruptly.)* Most of the time? What about the rest of the time?

HORNBY. You were taken for walks twice a week. We encouraged your legs to move. *(Pause.)* At other times you would suddenly move of your own volition very quickly, very quickly indeed, spasmodically, for short periods, and as suddenly as you began you would stop. *(Pause.)*

DEBORAH. Did you ever see ... tears ... well in my eyes?

HORNBY. No.

DEBORAH. And when I laughed ... did you laugh with me?

HORNBY. You never laughed.

DEBORAH. Of course I laughed. I have a laughing nature. *(Pause.)* Right. I'll get up now. *(He moves to her.)* No! Don't! Don't be ridiculous. *(She eases herself out of the bed, stands, falls. He moves to her.)* No! Don't! Don't! Don't! Don't touch me. *(She stands, very*

16

slowly. He retreats, watching. She stands still, begins to walk, in slow motion, towards him.) Let us dance. *(She dances, by herself, in slow motion.)* I dance. *(She dances.)* I've kept in practice, you know. I've been dancing in very narrow spaces. Kept stubbing my toes and bumping my head. Like Alice. Shall I sit here? I shall sit here. *(She sits at the table. He joins her. She touches the arms of her chair, touches the table, examines the table.)* I like tables, don't you? This is a rather beautiful table. Any chance of a dry sherry?

HORNBY. Not yet. Soon we'll have a party for you.

DEBORAH. A party? For me? How nice. Lots of cakes and lots of booze?

HORNBY. That's right.

DEBORAH. How nice. *(Pause.)* Well, it's nice at this table. What's the news? I suppose the war's still over?

HORNBY. It's over, yes.

DEBORAH. Oh good. They haven't started another one?

HORNBY. No.

DEBORAH. Oh good. *(Pause.)*

HORNBY. You danced in narrow spaces?

DEBORAH. Oh yes. The most crushing spaces, the most punishing spaces. That was tough going. Very difficult. Like dancing with someone dancing on your foot all the time, I mean *all* the time, on the same spot, just slam, slam, a big boot on your foot, not the most ideal kind of dancing, not by a long chalk. But sometimes the space opened and became light, sometimes it opened and I was so light, and when you feel so light you can dance till dawn and I danced till dawn night after night, night after night … for a time … I think … until … *(She has become aware of the figure of Pauline, standing in the room. She stares at her. Pauline is a woman in her early forties.)*

PAULINE. Deborah. *(Deborah stares at her.)* Deborah. It's Pauline. *(Pauline turns to Hornby.)* She's looking at me. *(She turns back to Deborah.)* You're looking at me. Oh Deborah … you haven't looked at me … for such a long time. *(Pause.)* I'm your sister. Do you know me? *(Deborah laughs shortly and turns away. Hornby stands and goes to Pauline.)*

HORNBY. I didn't call you. *(Pauline regards him.)* Well, all right. Speak to her.

PAULINE. What shall I say?

HORNBY. Just talk to her.

PAULINE. Doesn't it matter what I say?

17

HORNBY. No.

PAULINE. I can't do her harm?

HORNBY. No.

PAULINE. Shall I tell her lies or the truth?

HORNBY. Both. *(Pause.)*

PAULINE. You're trembling.

HORNBY. Am I?

PAULINE. Your hand.

HORNBY. Is it? *(He looks at his hand.)* Trembling? Is it? Yes. *(Pauline goes to Deborah, sits with her at the table.)*

PAULINE. Debby. I've spoken to the family. Everyone was so happy. I spoke to them all, in turn. They're away, you see. They're on a world cruise. They deserve it. It's been so hard for them. And Daddy's not too well, although in many respects he's as fit as a fiddle, and Mummy ... It's a wonderful trip. They passed through the Indian Ocean. And the Bay of Bosphorus. Can you imagine? Estelle also ... needed a total break. It's a wonderful trip. Quite honestly, it's the trip of a lifetime. They've stopped off in Bangkok. That's where I found them. I spoke to them all, in turn. And they all send so much love to you. Especially Mummy. *(Pause.)* I spoke by radio telephone. Shore to ship. The captain's cabin. Such excitement. *(Pause.)* Tell me. Do you ... remember me? *(Deborah stands and walks to her bed, in slow motion. Very slowly she gets into the bed. She lies against the pillows, closes her eyes. She opens her eyes, looks at Pauline, beckons to her. Pauline goes to the bed.)*

DEBORAH. Let me look into your eyes. *(She looks deeply into Pauline's eyes.)* So you say you're my sister?

PAULINE. I am.

DEBORAH. Well, you've changed. A great deal. You've aged ... substantially. What happened to you? *(Deborah turns to Hornby.)* What happened to her? Was it a sudden shock? I know shocks can age people overnight. Someone told me. *(She turns to Pauline.)* Is that what happened to you? Did a sudden shock age you overnight?

PAULINE. No it was you — *(Pauline looks at Hornby. He looks back at her, impassive. Pauline turns back to Deborah.)* It was you. You were standing with a vase of flowers in your hands. You were about to put it down on the table. But you didn't put it down. You stood still, with the vase in your hands, as if you were ... fixed. I was with you, in the room. I looked into your eyes. *(Pause.)* I said: "Debby?" *(Pause.)* But you remained ... quite ... still. I touched you. I said: "Debby?" Your eyes were open. You were looking nowhere. Then you suddenly looked at me and saw me and smiled at me and put the vase down on the table. *(Pause.)* But at the end of dinner, we were all laughing and talking, and Daddy was making jokes and making us laugh, and you said you couldn't see him properly because of the flowers in the middle of the table, where you had put them, and you stood and picked up the vase and you took it towards that little sidetable by the window, walnut, and Mummy was laughing and even Estelle was laughing and then we suddenly looked at you and you had stopped. You were standing with the vase by the sidetable, you were about to put it down, your arm was stretched towards it but you had stopped. *(Pause.)* We went to you. We spoke to you. Mummy touched you. She spoke to you. *(Pause.)* Then Daddy tried to take the vase from you. He could not … wrench it from your hands. He could not …move you from the spot. Like … marble. *(Pause.)* You were sixteen. *(Deborah turns to Hornby.)*

DEBORAH. She must be an aunt I never met. One of those distant cousins. *(To Pauline:)* Have you left me money in your Will? Well, I could do with it.

PAULINE. I'm Pauline.

DEBORAH. Well, if you're Pauline you've put on a remarkable amount of weight in a very short space of time. I can see you're not keeping up with your ballet classes. My God! You've grown breasts! *(Deborah stares at Pauline's breasts and suddenly looks down at herself.)*

PAULINE. We're women.

DEBORAH. Women?

PAULINE. You're a grown woman, Deborah.

DEBORAH. *(To Pauline:)* Is Estelle going to marry that ginger boy from Townley Street?

HORNBY. Deborah. Listen. You're not listening.

DEBORAH. To what?

HORNBY. To what your sister has been saying.

DEBORAH. *(To Pauline:)* Are you my sister?

PAULINE. Yes. Yes.

DEBORAH. But where did you get those breasts?

PAULINE. They came about. *(Deborah looks down at herself.)*

DEBORAH. I'm slimmer. Aren't I?

PAULINE. Yes.

DEBORAH. Yes. I'm slimmer. *(Pause.)* I'm going to run into the sea

19

and fall into the waves. I'm going to rummage about in all the water. *(Pause.)* Are we going out to dinner tonight? *(Pause.)* Where's Jack? Tongue-tied as usual. He's too shy for his own good. And Pauline's so sharp she'll cut herself. And Estelle's such a flibbertigibbet. I think she should marry that ginger boy from Townley Street and settle down before it's too late. *(Pause.)*

PAULINE. I am a widow.

DEBORAH. This woman is mad.

HORNBY. No. She's not. *(Pause.)* She has been coming to see you regularly … for a long time. She has suffered for you. She has never forsaken you. Nor have I. *(Pause.)* I have been your doctor for many years. This is your sister. Your father is blind. Estelle looks after him. She never married. Your mother is dead. *(Pause.)* It was I who took the vase from your hands. I lifted you onto this bed, like a corpse. Some wanted to bury you. I forbade it. I have nourished you, watched over you, for all this time. *(Pause.)* I injected you and woke you up. You will ask why I did not inject you twenty-nine years ago. I'll tell you. I did not possess the appropriate fluid. *(Pause.)* You see, you have been nowhere, absent, indifferent. It is we who have suffered. *(Pause.)* You do see that, I'm sure. You were an extremely intelligent young girl. All opinions confirm this. Your mind has not been damaged. It was merely suspended, it took up a temporary habitation … in a kind of Alaska. But it was not entirely static, was it? You ventured into quite remote … utterly foreign … territories. You kept on the move. And I charted your itinerary. Or did my best to do so. I have never let you go. *(Silence.)* I have never let you go. *(Silence.)* I have lived with you. *(Pause.)* Your sister Pauline was twelve when you were left for dead. When she was twenty I married her. She is a widow. I have lived with you. *(Silence.)*

DEBORAH. I want to go home. *(Pause.)* I'm cold. *(She takes Pauline's hand.)* Is it my birthday soon? Will I have a birthday party? Will everyone be there? will they all come? All our friends? How old will I be?

PAULINE. You will. You will have a birthday party. And everyone will be there. All your family will be there. All your old friends. And we'll have presents for you. All wrapped up … wrapped up in such beautiful paper.

DEBORAH. What presents?

PAULINE. Ah, we're not going to tell you. We're not going to tell you that. Because they're a secret. *(Pause.)* Think of it. Think of the thrill … of opening them, of unwrapping them, of taking out your presents and looking at them.

DEBORAH. Can I keep them?

PAULINE. Of course you can keep them. They're your presents. They're for you…only.

DEBORAH. I might lose them.

PAULINE. No, no. We'll put them all around you in your bedroom. We'll see that nobody else touches them. Nobody will touch them. And we'll kiss you goodnight. And when you wake up in the morning your presents … *(Pause.)*

DEBORAH. I don't want to lose them.

PAULINE. They'll never be lost. Ever. *(Pause.)* And we'll sing to you. What will we sing?

DEBORAH. What?

PAULINE. We'll sing "Happy Birthday" to you. *(Pause.)*

DEBORAH. Now what was I going to say? *(She begins to flick her cheek, as if brushing something from it.)* Now what — ? Oh dear, oh no. Oh dear. *(Pause.)* Oh dear. *(The flicking of her cheek grows faster.)* Yes, I think they're closing in. They're closing in. They're closing the walls in. Yes. *(She bows her head, flicking faster, her fingers now moving about over her face.)* Oh … well … oooohhhhh … oh no … oh no … *(During the course of this speech her body becomes hunchbacked.)* Let me out. Stop it. Let me out. Stop it. Stop it. Stop it. Shutting the walls on me. Shutting them down on me. So tight, so tight. Something panting, something panting. Can't see. Oh, the light is going. The light is going. They're shutting up shop. They're closing my face. Chains and padlocks. Bolting me up. Stinking. The smell. Oh my goodness, oh dear, oh my goodness, oh dear, I'm so young. It's a vice. I'm in a vice. It's at the back of my neck. Ah. Eyes stuck. Only see the shadow of the tip of my nose. Shadow of the tip of my nose. Eyes stuck. *(She stops flicking abruptly, sits still. Her body straightens. She looks up. She looks at her fingers, examines them.)* Nothing. *(Silence. She speaks calmly, is quite still.)* Do you hear a drip? *(Pause.)* I hear a drip. Someone's left the tap on. *(Pause.)* I'll tell you what it is. It's a vast series of halls. With enormous interior windows masquerading as walls. The windows are mirrors, you see. And so glass reflects glass. For ever and ever. *(Pause.)* You can't imagine how still it is. So silent I hear my eyes move. *(Silence.)* I'm lying in bed. People bend over me, speak to me. I want to say hullo, to have a chat, to make some inquiries. But you can't do that if

21

you're in a vast hall of glass with a tap dripping. *(Silence. She looks at Pauline.)* I must be quite old. I wonder what I look like. But it's of no consequence. I certainly have no intention of looking into a mirror. *(Pause.)* No. *(She looks at Hornby.)* You say I have been asleep. You say I am now awake. You say I have not awoken from the dead. You say I was not dreaming then and am not dreaming now. You say I have always been alive and am alive now. You say I am a woman. *(She looks at Pauline, then back to Hornby.)* She is a widow. She doesn't go to her ballet classes any more. Mummy and Daddy and Estelle are on a world cruise. They've stopped off in Bangkok. It'll be my birthday soon. I think I have the matter in proportion. *(Pause.)* Thank you.

End of Play

VICTORIA STATION

CHARACTERS

CONTROLLER
DRIVER

VICTORIA STATION

Lights up on office. Controller sitting at microphone.

CONTROLLER. 274? Where are you? *(Lights up on Driver in car.)* 274? Where are you? *(Pause.)*

DRIVER. Hullo?

CONTROLLER. 274?

DRIVER. Hullo?

CONTROLLER. Is that 274?

DRIVER. That's me.

CONTROLLER. Where are you?

DRIVER. What? *(Pause.)*

CONTROLLER. I'm talking to 274? Right?

DRIVER. Yes. That's me. I'm 274. Who are you? *(Pause.)*

CONTROLLER. Who am I?

DRIVER. Yes.

CONTROLLER. Who do you think I am? I'm your office.

DRIVER. Oh yes.

CONTROLLER. Where are you?

DRIVER. I'm cruising.

CONTROLLER. What do you mean? *(Pause.)* Listen son. I've got a job for you. If you're in the area I think you're in. Where are you?

DRIVER. I'm just cruising about.

CONTROLLER. Don't cruise. Stop cruising. Nobody's asking you to cruise about. What the fuck are you cruising about for? *(Pause.)* 274?

DRIVER. Hullo. Yes. That's me.

CONTROLLER. I want you to go to Victoria Station. I want you to pick up a customer coming from Boulogne. That is what I want you to do. Do you follow me? Now the question I want to ask you is this. Where are you? And don't say you're just cruising about. Just tell me if you're anywhere near Victoria Station.

DRIVER. Victoria what? *(Pause.)*

CONTROLLER. Station. *(Pause.)* Can you help me on this?

DRIVER. Sorry?

CONTROLLER. Can you help me on this? Can you come to my aid on this? *(Pause.)* You see, 274, I've got no-one else in the area, you see. I've only got you in the area. I think. Do you follow me?

DRIVER. I follow you, yes.

CONTROLLER. And this is a good job, 274. He wants you to take him to Cuckfield.

DRIVER. Eh?

CONTROLLER. He wants you to take him to Cuckfield. You're meeting the 10:22 from Boulogne. The European Special. His name's MacRooney. He's a little bloke with a limp. I've known him for years. You pick him up under the clock. You'll know him by his hat. He'll have a hat on with a feather in it. He'll be carrying fishing tackle. 274?

DRIVER. Hullo?

CONTROLLER. Are you hearing me?

DRIVER. Yes. *(Pause.)*

CONTROLLER. What are you doing?

DRIVER. I'm not doing anything.

CONTROLLER. How's your motor? Is your motor working?

DRIVER. Oh yes.

CONTROLLER. Your ignition's not on the blink?

DRIVER. No.

CONTROLLER. So you're sitting in a capable car?

DRIVER. I'm sitting in it, yes.

CONTROLLER. Are you in the driving seat? *(Pause.)* Do you understand what I mean? *(Pause.)* Do you have a driving wheel in front of you? *(Pause.)* Because I haven't, 274. I'm just talking into this machine, trying to make some sense out of our lives. That's my function. God gave me this job. He asked me to do this job, personally. I'm your local monk, 274. I'm a monk. You follow? I lead a restricted life. I haven't got a choke and a gear lever in front of me. I haven't got a cooling system and four wheels. I'm not sitting here with wing mirrors and a jack in the boot. And if I did have a jack in the boot I'd stick it right up your arse. *(Pause.)* Listen, 274. I've got every reason to believe that you're driving a Ford Cortina. I would very much like you to go to Victoria Station. *In* it. That means I don't want you to walk down there. I want you to drive down there. Right?

DRIVER. Everything you say is correct. This is a Ford Cortina.

CONTROLLER. Good. That's right. And you're sitting in it while we're having this conversation, aren't you?

DRIVER. That's right.

CONTROLLER. Where?

DRIVER. By the side of a park.

CONTROLLER. By the side of a park?

DRIVER. Yes.

CONTROLLER. What park?

DRIVER. A dark park.

CONTROLLER. Why is it dark? *(Pause.)*

DRIVER. That's not an easy question. *(Pause.)*

CONTROLLER. Isn't it?

DRIVER. No. *(Pause.)*

CONTROLLER. You remember this customer I was talking to you about? The one who's coming in to Victoria Station? Well, he's very keen for you to take him down to Cuckfield. He's got an old aunt down there. I've got a funny feeling she's going to leave him all her plunder. He's going down to pay his respects. He'll be in a good mood. If you play your cards right you might come out in front. Get me? *(Pause.)* 274?

DRIVER. Yes? I'm here.

CONTROLLER. Go to Victoria Station.

DRIVER. I don't know it.

CONTROLLER. You don't know it?

DRIVER. No. What is it? *(Silence.)*

CONTROLLER. It's a station, 274. *(Pause.)* Haven't you heard of it?

DRIVER. No. Never. What kind of place is it? *(Pause.)*

CONTROLLER. You've never heard of Victoria Station?

DRIVER. Never. No.

CONTROLLER. It's a famous station.

DRIVER. Well, I honestly don't know what I've been doing all these years.

CONTROLLER. What have you been doing all these years?

DRIVER. Well, I honestly don't know. *(Pause.)*

CONTROLLER. All right 274. Report to the office in the morning. 135? Where are you? 135? Where are you?

DRIVER. Don't leave me.

CONTROLLER. What? Who's that?

DRIVER. It's me. 274. Please. Don't leave me.

CONTROLLER. 135? Where are you?

DRIVER. Don't have anything to do with 135. He's not your man. He'll lead you into blind alleys by the dozen. They all will. Don't leave me. I'm your man. I'm the only one you can trust. *(Pause.)*

CONTROLLER. Do I know you, 274? Have we met? *(Pause.)* Well, it'll be nice to meet you in the morning. I'm really looking forward to it. I'll be sitting here with my cat o'nine tails, son. And you know what I'm going to do with it? I'm going to tie you up bollock naked to a butcher's table and I'm going to flog you to death all the way to Crystal Palace.

DRIVER. That's where I am! I knew I knew the place. *(Pause.)* I'm sitting by a little dark park underneath Crystal Palace. I can see the Palace. It's silhouetted against the sky. It's a wonderful edifice, isn't it? *(Pause.)* My wife's in bed. Probably asleep. And I've got a little daughter.

CONTROLLER. Oh, you've got a little daughter? *(Pause.)*

DRIVER. Yes, I think that's what she is.

CONTROLLER. Report to the office at 9 a.m. 135? Where are you? Where the fuck is 135? 246? 178? 101? Will somebody help me? Where's everyone gone? I've got a good job going down to Cuckfield. Can anyone hear me?

DRIVER. I can hear you.

CONTROLLER. Who's that?

DRIVER. 274. Here. Waiting. What do you want me to do?

CONTROLLER. You want to know what I want you to do?

DRIVER. Oh by the way, there's something I forgot to tell you.

CONTROLLER. What is it?

DRIVER. I've got a P.O.B.

CONTROLLER. You've got a P.O.B.?

DRIVER. Yes. That means passenger on board.

CONTROLLER. I know what it means, 274. It means you've got a passenger on board.

DRIVER. That's right.

CONTROLLER. You've got a passenger on board sitting by the side of a park?

DRIVER. That's right.

CONTROLLER. Did I book this job?

DRIVER. No, I don't think you came into it.

CONTROLLER. Well, where does he want to go?

DRIVER. He doesn't want to go anywhere. We just cruised about for a bit and then we came to rest.

CONTROLLER. In Crystal Palace?

DRIVER. Not *in* the Palace.

CONTROLLER. Oh, you're not *in* the Palace?

DRIVER. No. I'm not right inside it.

CONTROLLER. I think you'll find the Crystal Palace burnt down years ago, old son. It burnt down in the Great Fire of London. *(Pause.)*

DRIVER. Did it?

CONTROLLER. 274?

DRIVER. Yes. I'm here.

CONTROLLER. Drop your passenger. Drop your passenger at his chosen destination and proceed to Victoria Station. Otherwise I'll destroy you bone by bone. I'll chew your stomach out with my own teeth. I'll eat all the hair off your body. You'll end up looking like a pipe cleaner. Get me? *(Pause.)* 274? *(Pause.)* You're beginning to obsess me. I think I'm going to die. I'm alone in this miserable freezing fucking office and nobody loves me. Listen, pukeface —

DRIVER. Yes? *(Pause.)*

CONTROLLER. 135? 135? Where are you?

DRIVER. Don't have anything to do with 135. They're all bloodsuckers. I'm the only one you can trust. *(Pause.)*

CONTROLLER. You know what I've always dreamed of doing? I've always had this dream of having a holiday in sunny Barbados. I'm thinking of taking this holiday at the end of this year, 274. I'd like you to come with me. To Barbados. Just the two of us. I'll take you snorkelling. We can swim together in the blue Caribbean. *(Pause.)* In the meantime, though, why don't you just pop back to the office now and I'll make you a nice cup of tea? You can tell me something about your background, about your ambitions and aspirations. You can tell me all about your little hobbies and pastimes. Come over and have a nice cup of tea, 274.

DRIVER. I'd love to but I've got a passenger on board.

CONTROLLER. Put your passenger on to me. Let me have a word with him.

DRIVER. I can't. She's asleep on the back seat.

CONTROLLER. She?

DRIVER. Can I tell you a secret?

CONTROLLER. Please do.

DRIVER. I think I've fallen in love. For the first time in my life.

CONTROLLER. Who have you fallen in love with?

DRIVER. With this girl on the back seat. I think I'm going to keep her for the rest of my life. I'm going to stay in this car with her for the rest of my life. I'm going to marry her in this car. We'll die together in this car. *(Pause.)*

CONTROLLER. So you've found true love at last, eh, 274?

DRIVER. Yes. I've found true love at last.

CONTROLLER. So you're a happy man now then, are you?

DRIVER. I'm very happy. I've never known such happiness.

CONTROLLER. Well, I'd like to be the first to congratulate you, 274. I'd like to extend my sincere felicitations to you.

DRIVER. Thank you very much.

CONTROLLER. Don't mention it. I'll have to make a note in my diary not to forget your Golden Wedding, won't I? I'll bring along some of the boys to drink your health. Yes, I'll bring along some of the boys. We'll all have a few jars and a bit of a sing-song. *(Pause.)* 274? *(Pause.)*

DRIVER. Hullo. Yes. It's me.

CONTROLLER. Listen. I've been thinking. I've decided that what I'd like to do now is come down there and shake you by the hand straightaway. I'm going to shut this little office and I'm going to jump into my old car and I'm going to pop down to see you, to shake you by the hand. All right?

DRIVER. Fine. But what about this man coming off the train at Victoria Station — the 10:22 from Boulogne?

CONTROLLER. He can go and fuck himself.

DRIVER. I see.

CONTROLLER. No, I'd like to meet your lady friend, you see. And we can have a nice celebration. Can't we? So just stay where you are. Right? *(Pause.)* Right? *(Pause.)* 274?

DRIVER. Yes?

CONTROLLER. Don't move. Stay exactly where you are. I'll be right with you.

DRIVER. No, I won't move. *(Silence.)* I'll be here. *(Light out in office. The Driver sits still. Light out in car.)*

End of Play

FAMILY VOICES

CHARACTERS

VOICE 1 — a young man

VOICE 2 — a woman

VOICE 3 — a man

FAMILY VOICES was first broadcast on BBC Radio 3 on 22 January 1981.
The cast was as follows:

VOICE 1 ....Michael Kitchen
VOICE 2 ....Peggy Ashcroft
VOICE 3 .... Mark Dignam

Director Peter Hall

FAMILY VOICES was subsequently presented in a "platform performance" by the National Theatre, London, on 13 February 1981. Cast and director were the same. The décor was by John Bury.

FAMILY VOICES

VOICE 1. I am having a very nice time.

The weather is up and down, but surprisingly warm, on the whole, more often than not.

I hope you're feeling well, and not as peaky as you did, the last time I saw you.

No, you didn't feel peaky, you felt perfectly well, you simply looked peaky.

Do you miss me?

I am having a very nice time and I hope you are glad of that.

At the moment I am dead drunk.

I had five pints in The Fishmongers Arms tonight, followed by three double scotches, and literally rolled home.

When I say home I can assure you that my room is extremely pleasant. So is the bathroom. Extremely pleasant. I have some very pleasant baths indeed in the bathroom. So does everybody else in the house. They all lie quite naked in the bath and have very pleasant baths indeed. All the people in the house go about saying what a superb bath and bathroom the one we share is, they go about telling literally everyone they meet what lovely baths you can get in this place, more or less unparalleled, to put it bluntly.

It's got a lot to do with the landlady, who is a Mrs Withers, a person who turns out to be an utterly charming person, of impeccable credentials.

When I said I was drunk I was of course making a joke.

I bet you laughed.

Mother?

Did you get the joke? You know I never touch alcohol.

I like being in this enormous city, all by myself. I expect to make friends in the not too distant future.

I expect to make girlfriends too.

I expect to meet a very nice girl. Having met her, I shall bring her home to meet my mother.

I like walking in this enormous city, all by myself. It's fun to know no-one at all. When I pass people in the street they don't realise that I don't know them from Adam. They know other people and even more other people know them, so they naturally think that even if I don't know them I know the other people. So they look at me, they try to catch my eye, they expect me to speak. But as I do not know them I do not speak. Nor do I ever feel the slightest temptation to do so.

You see, mother, I am not lonely, because all that has ever happened to me is with me, keeps me company; my childhood, for example, through which you, my mother, and he, my father, guided me.

I get on very well with my landlady, Mrs Withers. She tells me I am her solace. I have a drink with her at lunchtime and another one at teatime and then take her for a couple in the evening at The Fishmongers Arms.

She was in the Women's Air Force in the Second World War. Don't drop a bollock, Charlie, she's fond of saying, Call him Flight Sergeant and he'll be happy as a pig in shit.

You'd really like her, mother.

I think it's dawn. I can see it coming up. Another day. A day I warmly welcome. And so I shall end this letter to you, my dear mother, with my love.

VOICE 2. Darling. Where are you? The flowers are wonderful here. The blooms. You so loved them. Why do you never write?

I think of you and wonder how you are. Do you ever think of me? Your mother? Ever? At all?

Have you changed your address?

Have you made friends with anyone? A nice boy? Or a nice girl?

There are so many nice boys and nice girls about. But please don't get mixed up with the other sort. They can land you in such terrible trouble. And you'd hate it so. You're so scrupulous, so particular.

I often think that I would love to live happily ever after with you and your young wife. And she would be such a lovely wife to you and I would have the occasional dinner with you both. A dinner I would be quite happy to cook myself, should you both be tired after your long day, as I'm sure you will be.

I sometimes walk the cliff path and think of you. I think of the times you walked the cliff path, with your father, with cheese sandwiches. Didn't you? You both sat on the clifftop and ate my cheese sandwiches together. Do you remember our little joke? Munch, munch. We had a damn good walk, your father would say. You mean you had a good munch munch, I would say. And you would both laugh.

Darling. I miss you. I gave birth to you. Where are you?

I wrote to you three months ago, telling you of your father's death. Did you receive my letter?

VOICE 1. I'm not at all sure that I like the people in this house, apart from Mrs Withers and her daughter, Jane. Jane is a schoolgirl who works hard at her homework.

35

She keeps her nose to the grindstone. This I find impressive. There's not too much of that about these days. But I'm not so sure about the other people in this house.

One is an old man.

The one who is an old man retires early. He is bald.

The other is a woman who wears red dresses.

The other one is another man.

He is big. He is much bigger than the other man. His hair is black. He has black eyebrows and black hair on the back of his hands.

I ask Mrs Withers about them but she will talk of nothing but her days in the Women's Air Force in the Second World War.

I have decided that Jane is not Mrs Withers' daughter but her grand-daughter. Mrs Withers is seventy. Jane is fifteen. That I am convinced is the truth.

At night I hear whispering from the other rooms and do not understand it. I hear steps on the stairs but do not dare go out to investigate.

VOICE 2. As your father grew closer to his death he spoke more and more of you, with tenderness and bewilderment. I consoled him with the idea that you had left home to make him proud of you. I think I succeeded in this. One of his last sentences was: Give him a slap on the back from me. Give him a slap on the back from me.

VOICE 1. I have made a remarkable discovery. The old man who is bald and who retires early is named Withers. Benjamin Withers. Unless it is simply a coincidence it must mean that he is a relation.

I asked Mrs Withers what the truth of this was. She poured herself a gin and looked at it before she drank it. Then she looked at me and said: You are my little pet. I've always wanted a little pet but I've never had one and now I've got one.

Sometimes she gives me a cuddle, as if she were my mother.

But I haven't forgotten that I have a mother and that you are my mother.

VOICE 2. Sometimes I wonder if you remember that you have a mother.

VOICE 1. Something has happened. The woman who wears red dresses stopped me and asked me into her room for a cup of tea. I went into her room. It was far bigger than I had expected, with sofas and curtains and veils and shrouds and rugs and soft material all over the walls, dark blue. Jane was sitting on a sofa doing her homework, by the look of it. I was invited to sit on the same sofa. Tea had already been made and stood ready, in a china teaset, of a most elegant design. I was given a cup. So was Jane, who smiled at me. I haven't introduced myself, the woman said, my name is Lady Withers. Jane sipped her tea with her legs up on the sofa. Her stockinged toes came to rest on my thigh. It wasn't the biggest sofa in the world. Lady Withers sat opposite us on a substantially bigger sofa. Her dress, I decided, wasn't red but pink. Jane was in green, apart from her toes, which were clad in black. Lady Withers asked me about you, mother. She asked me about my mother. I said, with absolute conviction, that you were the best mother in the world. She asked me to call her Lally. And to call Jane Jane. I said I did call Jane Jane. Jane gave me a bun. I think it was a bun. Lady Withers bit into her bun. Jane bit into her bun, her toes now resting on my lap. Lady Withers seemed to be enjoying her bun, on her sofa. She finished it and picked up another. I had never seen so many buns. One quick glance told me they were perched on cakestands, all over the room. Lady Withers went through her second bun with no trouble at all and was at once on to another. Jane, on the other hand, chewed almost dreamily at her bun and when a currant was left stranded on her upper lip she licked it off, without haste. I could not reconcile this with the fact that her toes were quite restless, even agitated. Her mouth, eating, was measured, serene; her toes, not eating, were agitated, highly strung, some would say hysterical. My bun turned out to be rock solid. I bit into it, it jumped out of my mouth and bounced into my lap. Jane's feet caught it. It calmed her toes down. She juggled the bun, with some expertise, along them. I recalled that, in an early exchange between us, she had told me she wanted to be an acrobat.

VOICE 2. Darling. Where are you? Why do you never write? Nobody knows your whereabouts. Nobody knows if you are alive or dead. Nobody can find you. Have you changed your name?

If you are alive you are a monster. On his deathbed your father cursed you. He cursed me too, to tell the truth. He cursed everyone in sight. Except that you were not in sight. I do not blame you entirely for your father's ill humour, but your absence and silence were a great burden on him, a weariness to him. He died in lamentation and oath. Was that your wish? Now I am alone, apart from Millie, who sometimes comes over from Dover. She is some consolation. Her eyes well with tears when she speaks of you, your dear sister's eyes well with tears. She has made a truly happy marriage and has a lovely little boy. When he is older he will want to know where his uncle is. What shall we say?

Or perhaps you will arrive here in a handsome new car, one day, in the not too distant future, in a nice new suit, quite out of the blue, and hold me in your arms.

VOICE 1. Lady Withers stood up. As Jane is doing her homework, she said, perhaps you would care to leave and come again another day. Jane withdrew her feet, my bun clasped between her two big toes. Yes of course, I said, unless Jane would like me to help her with her homework. No thank you, said Lady Withers, I shall help her with her homework.

What I didn't say is that I am thinking of offering myself out as a tutor. I consider that I would make an excellent tutor, to the young, in any one of a number of subjects. Jane would be an ideal pupil. She possesses a true love of learning. That is the sense of her one takes from her every breath, her every sigh and exhalation. When she turns her eyes upon you you see within her eyes, raw, untutored, unexercised but willing, a deep love of learning.

These are midnight thoughts, mother, although the time is ten twenty-three, precisely.

VOICE 2. Darling?

VOICE 1. While I was lying in my bath this afternoon, thinking on these things, there was apparently a knock on the front door. The man with black hair apparently opened the door. Two women stood on the doorstep. They said they were my mother and my sister, and asked for me. He denied knowledge of me. No, he had not heard of me. No, there was no-one of that name resident. This was a family house, no strangers admitted. No, they got on very well, thank you very much, without intruders. I suggest, he said, that you both go back to where you come from, and stop bothering innocent hardworking people with your slanders and your libels, these all too predictable excrescences of the depraved mind at the end of its tether. I can smell your sort a mile off and I am quite prepared to put you both on a charge of malicious mischief, insulting behavior and vagabondage, in other words wandering around on doorsteps knowingly, without any visible means of support. So piss off out of it before I call a copper.

I was lying in my bath when the door opened. I thought I had locked it. My name's Riley, he said, How's the bath? Very nice, I said. You've got a wellknit yet slender frame, he said, I thought you only a snip, I never imagined you would be as wellknit and slender as I now see you are. Oh thank you, I said. Don't thank me, he said, It's God you have to thank. Or your mother. I've just dismissed a couple of imposters at the front door. We'll get no more shit from that quarter. He then sat on the edge of the bath and recounted to me what I've just recounted to you.

It interests me that my father wasn't bothered to make the trip.

VOICE 2. I hear your father's step on the stair. I hear his cough. But his step and his cough fade. He does not open the door.

Sometimes I think I have always been sitting like this. I sometimes think I have always been sitting like this, alone by an indifferent fire, curtains closed, night, winter.

You see, I have my thoughts too. Thoughts no-one else knows I have, thoughts none of my family ever knew I had. But I write of them to you now, wherever you are.

What I mean is that when, for example, I was washing your hair, with the most delicate shampoo, and rinsing, and then drying your hair so gently with my soft towel, so that no murmur came from you, of discomfort or unease, and then looked into your eyes, and saw you look into mine, knowing that you wanted no-one else, no-one at all, knowing that you were entirely happy in my arms, I knew also, for example, that I was at the same time sitting by an indifferent fire, alone in winter, in eternal night without you.

VOICE 1. Lady Withers plays the piano. They were sitting, the three women, about the room. About the room were bottles of a vin rosé, of a pink I shall never forget. They sipped their wine from such lovely glass, an elegance of gesture and grace I thought long dead. Lady Withers wore a necklace around her alabaster neck, a neck amazingly young. She played Schumann. She smiled at me. Mrs Withers and Jane smiled at me. I took a seat. I took it and sat in it. I am in it. I will never leave it.

Oh mother, I have found my home, my family. Little did I ever dream I could know such happiness.

VOICE 2. Perhaps I should forget all about you. Perhaps I should curse you as your father cursed you. Oh I pray, I pray your life is a torment to you. I wait for your letter begging me to come to you. I'll spit on it.

VOICE 1. Mother, mother, I've had the most unpleasant, the most mystifying encounter, with the man who calls himself Mr Withers. Will you give me your advice?

Come in here, son, he called. Look sharp. Don't mess about. I haven't got all night. I went in. A jug. A basin. A bicycle.

You know where you are? he said. You're in my room. It's not Euston station. Get me? It's a true oasis.

This is the only room in this house where you can pick up a caravanserai to all points West. Compris? Comprende? Get me? Are you prepared to follow me down the mountain? Look at me. My name's Withers. I'm there or thereabouts. Follow? Embargo on all duff terminology. With me? Embargo on all things redundant. All areas in that connection verboten. You're in a diseaseridden land, boxer. Keep your weight on all the left feet you can lay your hands on. Keep dancing. The old foxtrot is the classical response but that's not the response I'm talking about. Nor am I talking about the other response. Up the slaves. Get me? This is a place of creatures, up and down stairs. Creatures of the rhythmic splits, the rhythmic sideswipes, the rums and roulettes, the macaroni tatters, the dumplings in jam mayonnaise, a catapulting ordure of gross and ramshackle shenanigans, openended paraphernalia. Follow me? It all adds up. It's before you and behind you. I'm the only saviour of the grace you find yourself wanting in. Mind how you go. Look sharp. Get my drift? Don't let it get too mouldy. Watch the mould. Get the feel of it, sonny, get the density. Look at me.

And I did.

VOICE 2. I am ill.

VOICE 1. It was like looking into a pit of molten lava, mother. One look was enough for me.

VOICE 2. Come to me.

VOICE 1. I joined Mrs Withers for a Campari and soda in the kitchen. She spoke of her youth. I was a right titbit, she said. I was like a piece of plum duff. They used to come from miles to try their luck. I fell head over heels with a man in the Fleet Air Arm. He adored me. They had him murdered because they didn't want us to know happiness. I could have married him and had tons of sons. But oh no. He went down with his ship. I heard it on the wireless.

VOICE 2. I wait for you.

VOICE 1. Later that night Riley and I shared a cup of cocoa in his quarters. I like slender lads, Riley said. Slender but strong. I've never made any secret of it. But I've had to restrain myself, I've had to keep a tight rein on my inclinations. That's because my deepest disposition is towards religion. I've always been a deeply religious man. You can imagine the tension this creates in my soul. I walk about in a constant state of spiritual, emotional, psychological and physical tension. It's breathtaking, the discipline I'm called upon to exert. My lust is unimaginably violent but goes against my best interests, which are to keep on the right side of God. I'm a big man, as you see, I could crush a slip of a lad such as you to death, I mean the death that is love, the death I understand love to be. But meet it is that I keep those desires shackled in handcuffs and legirons. I'm good at that sort of thing because I'm a policeman by trade. And I'm highly respected. I'm highly respected both in the force and in church. The only place where I'm not highly respected is in this house. They don't give a shit for me here. Although I've always been a close relation. Of a sort. I'm a fine tenor but they never invite me to sing. I might as well be living in the middle of the Sahara desert. There are too many women here, that's the trouble. And it's no use talking to Baldy. He's well away. He lives in another area, best known to himself. I like health and strength and intelligent conversation. That's why I took a fancy to you, chum, apart from the fact that I fancy you. I've got no-one to talk to. These women treat me like a leper. Even though I am a relation. Of a sort.

What relation?

Is Lady Withers Jane's mother or sister?

If either is the case why isn't Jane called Lady Jane Withers? Or perhaps she is. Or perhaps neither is the case? Or perhaps Mrs Withers is actually the Honourable Mrs Withers? But if that is the case what does that make Mr Withers? And which Withers is he anyway? I mean what relation is he to the rest of the Witherses? And who is Riley?

But if you find me bewildered, anxious, confused, uncertain and afraid, you also find me content. My life possesses shape. The house has a very warm atmosphere, as you have no doubt gleaned. And as you have no doubt noted from my account I talk freely to all its inhabitants, with the exception of Mr Withers, to whom no-one talks, to whom no-one refers, with evidently good reason. But I rarely leave the house. No-one seems to leave the house. Riley leaves the house but rarely. He must be a secret policeman. Jane continues to do a great deal of homework while not apparently attending any school. Lady Withers never leaves the house. She has guests. She receives guests. Those are the steps I hear on the stairs at night.

VOICE 3. I know your mother has written to you to tell you that I am dead. I am not dead. I am very far from being dead, although lots of people have wished me dead, from time immemorial, you especially. It is you who have prayed for my death, from time immemorial. I have heard your prayers. They ring in my ears. Prayers yearning for my death. But I am not dead.

Well, that is not entirely true, not entirely the case. I'm lying. I'm leading you up the garden path, I'm playing about, I'm having my bit of fun, that's what. Because I am dead. As dead as a doornail. I'm writing to you from my grave. A quick word for old time's sake. Just to keep in touch. An old hullo out of the dark. A last kiss from Dad.

I'll probably call it a day after this canter. Not much more to say. All a bit of a sweat. Why am I taking the trouble? Because of you, I suppose, because you were such a loving son. I'm smiling, as I lie in this glassy grave.

Do you know why I use the word glassy? Because I can see out of it.

Lots of love, son. Keep up the good work.

There's only one thing bothers me, to be quite frank. While there is, generally, absolute silence everywhere, absolute silence throughout all the hours, I still hear, occasionally, a dog barking. I hear this dog. Oh, it frightens me.

VOICE 1. They have decided on a name for me. They call me Bobo. Good morning, Bobo, they say, or, See you in the morning, Bobo, or, Don't drop a goolie, Bobo, or, Don't forget the diver, Bobo, or, Keep your eye on the ball, Bobo, or, Keep this side of the tramlines, Bobo, or, How's the lead in your pencil, Bobo, or, How's tricks in the sticks, Bobo, or, Don't get too much gum in your gumboots, Bobo.

The only person who does not call me Bobo is the old man. He calls me nothing. I call him nothing. I don't see him. He keeps to his room. I don't go near it. He is old and will die soon.

VOICE 2. The police are looking for you. You may remember that you are still under twenty-one. They have issued your precise description to all the organs. They will not rest, they assure me, until you are found. I have stated my belief that you are in the hands of underworld figures who are using you as a male prostitute. I have declared in my affidavit that you have never possessed any strength of character whatsoever and that you are palpably susceptible to even the most blatant form of flattery and blandishment. Women were your downfall, even as a nipper. I haven't forgotten Françoise the French maid or the woman who masqueraded under the title of governess, the infamous Miss Carmichael. You will be found, my boy, and no mercy will be shown to you.

VOICE 1. I'm coming back to you, mother, to hold you in my arms.

I am coming home.

I am coming also to clasp my father's shoulder. Where is the old boy? I'm longing to have a word with him. Where is he? I've looked in all the usual places, including the old summerhouse, but I can't find him. Don't tell me he's left home at his age? That would be inexpressibly skittish a gesture, on his part. What have you done with him, mother?

VOICE 2. I'll tell you what, my darling. I've given you up as a very bad job. Tell me one last thing. Do you think the word love means anything?

VOICE 1. I am on my way back to you. I am about to make the journey back to you. What will you say to me?

VOICE 3. I have so much to say to you. But I am quite dead. What I have to say to you will never be said.

ONE FOR THE ROAD

CHARACTERS

NICOLAS — Mid 40s
VICTOR — 30
GILA — 30
NICKY — 7

A ROOM.

ONE FOR THE ROAD

Nicolas at his desk. He sits still. He leans forward and speaks into a machine.

NICOLAS. Bring him in. *(He sits back. The door opens. Victor walks in, slowly. His clothes are torn. He is bruised. The door closes behind him.)* Hello! Good morning. How are you? Let's not beat about the bush. Anything but that. D'accord? You're a civilised man. So am I. Sit down. *(Victor slowly sits. Nicolas stands, walks over to him.)* What do you think this is? It's my finger. And this is my little finger. This is my big finger and this is my little finger. I wave my big finger in front of your eyes. Like this. And now I do the same with my little finger. I can also use both … at the same time. Like this. I can do absolutely anything I like. Do you think I'm mad? My mother did. *(He laughs.)* Do you think waving fingers in front of people's eyes is silly? I can see your point. You're a man of the highest intelligence. But would you take the same view if it was my boot — or my penis? Why am I so obsessed with eyes? Am I obsessed with eyes? Possibly. Not my eyes. Other people's eyes. The eyes of people who are brought to me here. They're so vulnerable. The soul shines through them. Are you a religious man? I am. Which side do you think God is on? I'm going to have a drink. *(He goes to sideboard, pours whisky.)* You're probably wondering where your wife is. She's in another room. *(He drinks.)* Goodlooking woman. *(He drinks.)* God, that was good. *(He pours another.)* Don't worry, I can hold my booze. *(He drinks.)* You may have noticed I'm the chatty type. You probably think I'm part of a predictable, formal, long-established pattern; i.e. I chat away, friendly, insouciant, I open the batting, as it were, in a lighthearted, even carefree manner, while another waits in the wings, silent, introspective, coiled like a puma. No, no. it's not quite like that. I run the place. God speaks through me. I'm referring to the Old Testament God, by the way, although I'm a long way from being Jewish. Everyone respects me here. Including you, I take it? I think that is the correct stance. *(Pause.)* Stand up. *(Victor stands.)* Sit down. *(Victor sits.)* Thank you so much. *(Pause.)* Tell me something ... *(Silence.)* What a goodlooking woman your wife is. You're a lucky man. Tell me ... one for the road, I think ... *(He pours whisky.)* You do respect me, I take it? *(He stands in front of Victor and looks down at him. Victor looks up.)* I would be right in assuming that? *(Silence.)*

VICTOR. *(Quietly.)* I don't know you.

NICOLAS. But you respect me.

VICTOR. I don't know you.

NICOLAS. Are you saying you don't respect me? *(Pause.)* Are you saying you would respect me if you knew me better? Would you like to know me better? *(Pause.)* Would you like to know me better?

VICTOR. What I would like ... has no bearing on the matter.

NICOLAS. Oh yes it has. *(Pause.)* I've heard so much about you. I'm terribly pleased to meet you. Well, I'm not sure that pleased is the right word. One has to be so scrupulous about language. Intrigued. I'm intrigued. Firstly because I've heard so much about you. Secondly because if you don't respect me you're unique. Everyone else knows the voice of God speaks through me. You're not a religious man, I take it? *(Pause.)* You don't believe in a guiding light? *(Pause.)* What then? *(Pause.)* So ... morally ... you flounder in wet shit. You know ... like when you've eaten a rancid omelette. *(Pause.)* I think I deserve one for the road. *(He pours, drinks.)* Do you drink whisky? *(Pause.)* I hear you have a lovely house. Lots of books. Someone told me some of my boys kicked it around a bit. Pissed on the rugs, that sort of thing. I wish they wouldn't do that. I do really. But you know what it's like — they have such responsibilities — and they feel them — they are constantly present — day and night — these responsibilities — and so, sometimes, they piss on a few rugs. You understand. You're not a fool. *(Pause.)* Is your son all right?

VICTOR. I don't know.

NICOLAS. Oh, I'm sure he's all right. What age is he ... seven ... or thereabouts? Big lad, I'm told. Nevertheless, silly of him to behave as he did. But is he all right?

VICTOR. I don't know.

NICOLAS. Oh, I'm sure he's all right. Anyway, I'll have a word with him later and find out. He's somewhere on the second floor,

48

I believe. *(Pause.)* Well now ... *(Pause.)* What do you say? Are we friends? *(Pause.)* I'm prepared to be frank, as a true friend should. I love death. What about you? *(Pause.)* What about you? Do you love death? Not necessarily your own. Others. The death of others. Do you love the death of others, or, at any rate, do you love the death of others as much as I do? *(Pause.)* Are you always so dull? I understand you enjoyed the cut and thrust of debate. *(Pause.)* Death. Death. Death. Death. As has been noted by the most respected authorities, it is beautiful. The purest, most harmonious thing there is. Sexual intercourse is nothing compared to it. *(He drinks.)* Talking about sexual intercourse ... *(He laughs wildly, stops.)* Does she ... fuck? Or does she...? Or does she ... like ... you know ... what? What does she like? I'm talking about your wife. Your *wife.* *(Pause.)* You know the old joke? Does she fuck? *(Heavily, in another voice:)* Does she fuck! *(He laughs.)* It's ambiguous, of course. It could mean she fucks like a rabbit or she fucks not at all. *(Pause.)* Well, we're all God's creatures. Even your wife. *(Pause.)* There is only one obligation. *To be honest.* You have no other obligation. Weigh that. In your mind. Do you know the man who runs this country? No? Well, he's a very nice chap. He took me aside the other day, last Wednesday, I think it was, he took me aside, at a reception, visiting dignitaries, he took *me* aside, *me,* and he said to me, he said, in what I can only describe as a hoarse whisper, Nic, he said, Nic (that's my name), Nic, if you ever come across anyone whom you have good reason to believe is getting on my tits, tell them one thing, tell them honesty is the best policy. The cheese was superb. Goat. One for the road. *(He pours.)* Your wife and I had a very nice chat but I couldn't help noticing she didn't look her best. She's probably menstruating. Women do that. *(Pause.)* You know, old chap, I do love other things, apart from death. So many things. Nature. Trees, things like that. A nice blue sky. Blossom. *(Pause.)* Tell me ... truly ... are you beginning to love me? *(Pause.)* I think your wife is. Beginning. She is beginning to fall in love with me. On the brink ... of doing so. The trouble is, I have rivals. Because everyone here has fallen in love with your wife. It's her eyes have beguiled them. Her soul, they say, shines through them. What's her name? Gila ... or something? *(Pause.)* Who would you prefer to be? You or me? *(Pause.)* I'd go for me if I were you. The trouble about you, although I grant your merits, is that you're on a losing wicket, while I can't put a foot wrong. Do you take my point? Ah God, let me confess, let me make a confession to you. I have never been more moved, in the whole of my life, as when — only the other day, last Friday, I believe — the man who runs this country announced to the country: We are all patriots, we are as one, we all share a common heritage. Except you, apparently. *(Pause.)* I feel a link, you see, a bond. I share a commonwealth of interest. I am not alone. I am not alone! *(Silence.)*

VICTOR. Kill me.

NICOLAS. What?

VICTOR. Kill me. *(Nicolas goes to him, puts his arm around him.)*

NICOLAS. What's the matter? *(Pause.)* What in heaven's name is the matter? *(Pause.)* Mmmnnn? *(Pause.)* You're probably just hungry. Or thirsty. Let me tell you something. I hate despair. I find it intolerable. The stink of it gets up my nose. It's a blemish. Despair, old fruit, is a cancer. It should be castrated. Indeed I've often found that that works. Chop the balls off and despair goes out the window. You're left with a happy man. Or a happy woman. Look at me. *(Victor does so.)* Your soul shines out of your eyes.

BLACKOUT

LIGHTS UP
Nicolas standing with a small boy.

NICOLAS. What is your name?

NICKY. Nicky.

NICOLAS. Really? How odd. *(Pause.)* Do you like cowboys and Indians?

NICKY. Yes. A bit.

NICOLAS. What do you really like?

NICKY. I like aeroplanes.

NICOLAS. Real ones or toy ones?

NICKY. I like both kinds of ones.

NICOLAS. Do you? *(Pause.)* Why do you like aeroplanes? *(Pause.)*

NICKY. Well … because they go so fast. Through the air. The real ones do.

NICOLAS. And the toy ones?

NICKY. I pretend they go as fast as the real ones do. *(Pause.)*

NICOLAS. Do you like your mummy and daddy? *(Pause.)* Do you like your mummy and daddy?
NICKY. Yes.
NICOLAS. Why? *(Pause.)* Why? *(Pause.)* Do you find that a difficult question to answer? *(Pause.)*
NICKY. Where's Mummy?
NICOLAS. You don't like your mummy and daddy?
NICKY. Yes. I do.
NICOLAS. Why? *(Pause.)* Would you like to be a soldier when you grow up?
NICKY. I don't mind.
NICOLAS. You don't? Good. You like soldiers. Good. But you spat at my soldiers and you kicked them. You attacked them.
NICKY. Were they your soldiers?
NICOLAS. They are your country's soldiers.
NICKY. I didn't like those soldiers.
NICOLAS. They don't like you either, my darling.

BLACKOUT

LIGHTS UP
Nicolas sitting. Gila standing. Her clothes are torn. She is bruised.

NICOLAS. When did you meet your husband?
GILA. When I was eighteen.
NICOLAS. Why?
GILA. Why?
NICOLAS. Why?
GILA. I just met him.
NICOLAS. Why?
GILA. I didn't plan it.
NICOLAS. Why not?
GILA. I didn't know him.
NICOLAS. Why not? *(Pause.)* Why not?
GILA. I didn't know him.
NICOLAS. Why not?
GILA. I met him.

NICOLAS. When?

GILA. When I was eighteen.

NICOLAS. Why?

GILA. He was in the room.

NICOLAS. Room? *(Pause.)* Room?

GILA. The same room.

NICOLAS. As what?

GILA. As I was.

NICOLAS. As I was?

GILA. *(Screaming.)* As I was.

NICOLAS. Room? What room?

GILA. A room.

NICOLAS. What room?

GILA. My father's room.

NICOLAS. Your father? What's your father got to do with it? *(Pause.)* Your *father*? How dare you? Fuckpig. *(Pause.)* Your father was a wonderful man. His country is proud of him. He's dead. He was a man of honour. He's dead. Are you prepared to defame, to debase, the memory of your father? Your father fought for his country. I knew him. I revered him. Everyone did. He believed in God. He didn't *think*, like you shitbags. He *lived*. He lived. He was iron and gold. He would die, he would die, he would die, for his country, for his God. And he did die, he died, he died, for his God. You turd. To spawn such a daughter. What a fate. Oh, poor, perturbed spirit, to be haunted forever by such scum and spittle. How do you dare speak of your father to me? I loved him, as if he were my own father. *(Silence.)* Where did you meet your husband?

GILA. In a street.

NICOLAS. What were you doing there?

GILA. Walking.

NICOLAS. What was he doing?

GILA. Walking. *(Pause.)* I dropped something. He picked it up.

NICOLAS. What did you drop?

GILA. The evening paper.

NICOLAS. You were drunk. *(Pause.)* You were drugged. *(Pause.)* You had absconded from your hospital.

GILA. I was not in a hospital.

NICOLAS. Where are you now? *(Pause.)* Where are you now? Do you think you are in a hospital? *(Pause.)* Do you think we have nuns upstairs? *(Pause.)* What do we have upstairs?

GILA. No nuns.

NICOLAS. What do we have?

GILA. Men.

NICOLAS. Have they been raping you? *(She stares at him.)* How many times? *(Pause.)* How many times have you been raped? *(Pause.)* How many times? *(He stands, goes to her, lifts his finger.)* This is my big finger. And this is my little finger. Look. I wave them in front of your eyes. Like this. How many times have you been raped?

GILA. I don't know.

NICOLAS. And you consider yourself a reliable witness? *(He goes to sideboard, pours drink, sits, drinks.)* You're a lovely woman. Well, you were. *(He leans back, drinks, sighs.)* Your son is … seven. He's a little prick. You made him so. You have taught him to be so. You had a choice. You could have encouraged him to be a good person. Instead, you encouraged him to be a little prick. You encouraged him to spit, to strike at soldiers of honour, soldiers of God. *(Pause.)* Oh well…in one way I suppose it's academic. *(Pause.)* You're of no interest to me. I might even let you out of here, in due course. But I should think you might entertain us all a little more before you go.

BLACKOUT

LIGHTS UP
Nicolas standing. Victor sitting. Victor is tidily dressed.

NICOLAS. How have you been? Surviving?

VICTOR. Yes.

NICOLAS. Yes?

VICTOR. Yes. Yes.

NICOLAS. Really? How?

VICTOR. Oh … *(Pause.)*

NICOLAS. I can't hear you.

VICTOR. It's my mouth.

NICOLAS. Mouth?

VICTOR. Tongue.

NICOLAS. What's the matter with it? *(Pause.)* What about a drink? One for the road. What do you say to a drink? *(He goes to bottle, pours two gasses, gives a glass to Victor.)* Drink up. It'll put lead

53

in your pencil. And then we'll find someone to take it out. *(He laughs.)* We can do that, you know. We have a first class brothel upstairs, on the sixth floor, chandeliers, the lot. They'll suck you in and blow you out in little bubbles. All volunteers. Their daddies are in our business. Which is, I remind you, to keep the world clean for God. Get me? Drink up. Drink up. Are you refusing to drink with me? *(Victor drinks. His head falls back.)* Cheers. *(Nicolas drinks.)* You can go. *(Pause.)* You can leave. We'll meet again, I hope. I trust we will always remain friends. Go out. Enjoy life. Be good. Love your wife. She'll be joining you in about a week, by the way. If she feels up to it. Yes. I feel we've both benefited from our discussions. *(Victor mutters.)* What? *(Victor mutters.)* What?

VICTOR. My son.

NICOLAS. Your son? Oh, don't worry about him. He was a little prick. *(Victor straightens and stares at Nicolas. Silence. Blackout.)*

End of Play

PROPERTY LISTS

A KIND OF ALASKA

White bed, with pillows & sheets
Table
Chairs (2)

VICTORIA STATION

Desk and chair
Microphone, on desk
Auto mock-up (seat, steering wheel, dashboard)

ONE FOR THE ROAD

Desk and chair
Intercom, on desk
Sideboard, with whiskey bottle and glasses

NOTES
(Use this space to make notes for your production)